U.S. Air Force

BY LINDA BOZZO

Amicus High Interest is an imprint of Amicus
P.O. Box 1329, Mankato, MN 56002
www.amicuspublishing.us

Library of Congress Cataloging-in-Publication Data
Bozzo, Linda.
 U.S. Air Force / by Linda Bozzo.
    pages cm. -- (Serving in the military)
 Includes index.
 Summary: "An introduction to what the US Air Force is,
what recruits do, and jobs soldiers could learn. Includes
descriptions of missions to rescue soldiers in Afghanistan and
battle wildfires in Colorado"--Provided by publisher.
 Audience: Grades K-3.
 ISBN 978-1-60753-391-7 (library binding) -- ISBN 978-1-
60753-439-6 (ebook)
1. United States. Air Force--Juvenile literature. I. Title.
 UG633.B6965 2014
 358.400973--dc23
                                        2013001425

Editor   Wendy Dieker
Series Designer   Kathleen Petelinsek
Page production   Red Line Editorial, Inc.

Photo Credits
Staff Sgt. Christopher Hubenthal/U.S. Air Force, cover; Staff
Sgt. Christopher Boitz/U.S. Air Force, 4; Senior Airman Tony
R. Ritter/U.S. Air Force, 7; Senior Airman Brett Clashman/U.S.
Air Force, 8; Airman 1st Class Tyler Prince/U.S. Air Force, 11;
Raymond McCoy/Defense Imagery, 12; Senior Airman Brett
Clashman/U.S. Air Force, 15; Staff Sgt. Quinton Russ/U.S.
Air Force, 16; Staff Sgt. Jonathan Snyder/Defense Imagery,
18; Master Sgt. Dan Richardson/U.S. Air Force, 21; Capt.
Teresa Sullivan/Defense Imagery, 22; Senior Airman Julianne
Showalter/U.S. Air Force, 25; Staff Sgt. Stacey Haga/U.S. Air
Force, 26; Senior Master Sgt. John Rohrer/U.S. Air Force, 28

Printed in Printed in the United States at Corporate Graphics
in North Mankato, Minnesota
5-2013 / 1150
10 9 8 7 6 5 4 3 2 1

Table of Contents

The U.S. Air Force trains hard.
They are ready to save the day.

The Air Force to the Rescue!

It is April 2011. An Army helicopter crashed in the Middle East. The pilots are stranded. The U.S. Air Force to the rescue! Rescue teams get into their helicopters. They rush to the crash site. But they are in the middle of a war. Enemies are all around. That does not stop the **airmen**. They are ready for action.

Pararescue jumpers (PJs) drop from the choppers. They run to the crash site. The airmen find both pilots. But only one pilot is alive. The enemies are shooting all around. They airmen need to get the pilots back to the chopper! Fast!

 What is a pararescue jumper (PJ)?

PJs slide down ropes
out of a chopper.

A PJ jumps out of a plane. PJs find and save
stranded soldiers.

7

The helicopters hover above the ground. A **hoist** pulls up the injured pilot and some PJs. The enemies keep shooting! They need to get out fast! The airmen lift the body of other pilot with the rest of the PJs. The choppers fly back to the base. Rescue complete!

A PJ practices rescuing a soldier with a hoist.

Learning the Ropes

The U.S. Air Force is always ready to fly. They act quickly to keep our country safe. Members work as a team in the air. They even work in outer space. But the first step when joining the air force is to go to basic training in Texas.

 How long is basic training?

U.S. Airmen are ready to fly when there is a job to do.

 A Air force basic training takes eight-and-a-half weeks. All training is done at Lackland Air Force Base in Texas.

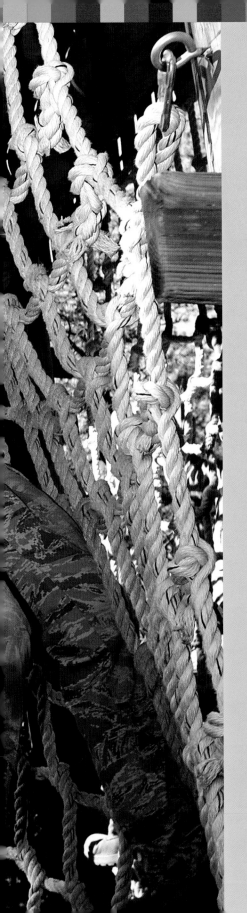

Trainees are called **recruits**. They work hard to keep fit. They learn how to fight in war. They learn to use weapons. They learn how to rescue other soldiers. Training also includes making camp in the wilderness. When recruits finish basic training they are called airmen. Even the women!

Airmen train hard!

13

After basic training, there are lots of jobs to learn. Some airmen learn how to launch missiles. Some learn how to jump out of a plane. Others train to become rescue pilots. Rescue pilots learn how to drop off and pick up rescue teams. Some airmen will be mechanics. Others will learn to use robots to blow up bombs so no one gets hurt.

This airman tightens wires on a fighter plane. It's an important job!

This airman helps inspect
a helicopter.

 How much training does it take
to be an officer?

Would you like to fly planes? How about handle bombs? Your job could be to jump out of a plane and rescue people. You might even fly planes to fight fires. There are security police who guard airfields. Maybe you would like to launch rockets into space. You might even become an officer. You could lead a team of airmen.

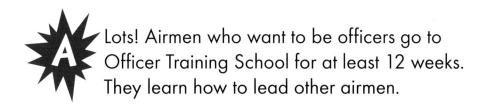

Lots! Airmen who want to be officers go to Officer Training School for at least 12 weeks. They learn how to lead other airmen.

The Home Front

On the home front, the U.S. Air Force's main job is to train to fight. But training is not their only job. Planes and helicopters need to be fueled and ready to fly at all times. Office workers order supplies. Pilots fly supplies to where they are needed.

Airmen load supplies onto a C-17 cargo plane.

The air force also works in outer space. Some airmen are astronauts. Other airmen launch spy **satellites**. They send off rockets and fire missiles across the ocean.

But there is one other very important job. It has nothing to do with fighting. That job is flying the president of the United States. The U.S. Air Force flies the president all over the world.

 Does the president have a special plane?

President Obama (left) gets off Air Force One.

 Yes. There are actually two planes ready for the president. The plane the president rides on is called Air Force One.

These airmen just finished a mission in Afghanistan.

Stationed Overseas

An air force job could take you to any part of the world. There are air bases in other countries. These bases keep planes and helicopters ready for action. Bases store supplies and have places for airmen to live. Each base has an airport. Airmen can fly to trouble quickly.

Overseas, the air force can be close to wars. Some airmen fly fighter jets. Fighter jets have missiles and machine guns. They fire at enemies on the ground and in the water. The air force works hard to keep people safe from enemies.

Flares from a U.S. gunship confuse enemy heat-seeking missiles.

Airmen give blankets to kids near a base overseas.

The U.S. Air Force helps countries in many ways. Airmen help people who live near their bases. They give children school supplies and toys. They also help after a disaster strikes. When **landslides** hit, the air force flies overhead. They drop food and water for the people. They also drop blankets and clothes.

An orange liquid is dropped on trees to help stop a wildfire.

 How big are the tanks on the planes?

Serving Our Country

It was June 2012 in Colorado. Wildfire!
Airmen got on planes with big tanks.
They flew very low over the fire. They
dropped streams of an orange liquid called
slurry. This helped stop the fire from
spreading. Soon the fire was out.

Whether fighting fires or battles, U.S.
Air Force members are heroes!

 Really big! You could fill about 75 bathtubs
with the water they can hold.

Glossary

airmen Air force recruits who have finished basic training; both men and women are called airmen.

hoist A piece of equipment used for lifting people.

landslide When a large amount of rocks or earth slip down a slope.

pararescue jumper (PJ) Someone who is trained to rescue people by jumping from a plane with a parachute.

recruit A person who has just joined the military.

satellite A piece of equipment in space used to spy on enemies.

slurry An orange liquid dropped from planes to help stop the spread of fire.

Read More

Aronin, Miriam. *Today's Air Force Heroes.* New York, NY. Bearport Publishing, 2012.

Goldish, Meish. *Air Force: Civilian to Airman.* New York, NY. Bearport Publishing, 2011.

Jackson, Kay. *Military Planes in Action.* New York, NY. PowerKids Press, 2009.

Websites

Air Force Services Child and Youth Programs
http://www.afyouthprograms.com/

Brain Pop: Social Studies: Learn About the Armed Forces
http://www.brainpop.com/socialstudies/ usgovernmentandlaw/armedforces/preview.weml

Official Site of the U.S. Air Force
http://www.af.mil/

Index

About the Author

Linda Bozzo is the author of more than 30 books for the school and library market. She would like to thank all of the men and women in the military for their outstanding service to our country. Visit Linda's website at www.lindabozzo.com.